AWAKEN
IN
OCTOBER
POEMS OF FOLK HORROR
AND HALLOWEEN

Praise for I Awaken in October

"Scott J. Couturier's poems are spirited paeans to the Season of the Pumpkin. With roots delving down into the fertile black earth, these agricultural incantations draw up the very primal sap whence autumn swells in all her fecund abundance. In these pages, as in nature, life fades into decay, and decay, a noxious bubbling cauldron, gives fungal fruit to new life—and so the Wheel turns. With all the sorcerous insight of a druid under nature's trance, this rare bard of grain and gourd takes us on a journey from spring's beginning to summer's end, and to the hibernal realm of dreams beyond. But when you awaken from that winter sleep, it may be that you will not awaken in the gladness of spring; it may be that you will awaken—once again—in October."

— **K. A. Opperman**, author of *Past the Glad and Sunlit Season: Poems for Halloween*

"*I Awaken in October* is a striking testimonial to the continued fascination of the season of autumn in our culture. In poems ranging from sonnets to free verse, Scott J. Couturier evokes the power of Nature and the weight of the past especially the primitive festivals of Samhain, Halloween, and the Yuletide as elements of terror that continue to resonate today. Dan Sauer's vivid illustrations are the perfect complement to the brooding dread that we find in every one of Scott's poetic vignettes."

— **S. T. Joshi**, editor of *Spectral Realms*

"Scott J. Couturier's *I Awaken in October* is a sublime poetic celebration of the shadow side of the year. Beginning with picturesque paeans to the season and its pagan observances, one is then grasped by the hair, joining Couturier in a nightmarish hayride through a haunted realm of infernal rites and yawning graveyards teeming with benighted spirits and fiendish beings. This book is a perfect read for those long autumnal nights, under a blanket by the hearth, with a mulled libation to ward off the eventide chill. Just remember to retain a burning candle as well, to keep the dark and its attendant entities at bay."

— **Manuel Arenas**, author of *Book of Shadows: Grim Tales and Gothic Fancies*

Praise for I Awaken in October

"From the fall of the leaves through harvest to hoarfrost, *I Awaken in October* is a fascinating journey through the autumnal regions of folklore and myth. Whether leading to celebratory rites or sombre woodland ceremonies, Couturier approaches each path with a sense of reverence for the season, which is here not so much a period of earthly time as it is an otherworldly place."

— **Wade German**, author of *Children of Hypnos, The Ladies of the Everlasting Lichen and Other Relics*, and *Dreams from a Black Nebula*

"The sensations of warm fiery rays of sunset and the ember-hued leaves crunching underfoot can be experienced in these scintillating verses by Scott J. Couturier in his debut poetry collection, *I Awaken in October*. Rich language and vivid descriptions are fine-tuned to capture the reader's imagination and attention. This book will make a fine addition any Halloween enthusiast's bookshelf."

— **Ashley Dioses**, author of *Diary of a Sorceress* and *The Withering*

"It's no secret a great gulf exists between modern civilization and the primeval world. Gone is our deep reverence, awe, and fear of nature, of mystery. Driven away are the fae. Let me reveal something about *I Awaken In October*. It's not just a book of dark, uncanny folk poems—it's a portal. And through it we perceive again, we course-correct the psyche. A brilliant, haunting collection that bridges the gap."

— **Jay Sturner**, naturalist and author of *The Hunchback's Captive and Others*

"Couturier's *I Awaken in October* is equal parts celebration, evocation, invocation, and incantation. Lyrical and lush, Couturier's poetry is a sensual immersion in the glories of autumn, the haunted forests of a pagan night, the marrow-deep chill of Yule, and the alchemical dance of the witch's hour. . . . Luxuriant, sumptuous, and exuberantly gothic."

— **Rebecca Buchanan**, author of *Asphalt Gods* and *Not A Princess, But (Yes) There Was A Pea & Other Fairy Tales To Foment Revolution*

Also by Scott J. Couturier

The Box

Also from Jackanapes Press

AVAILABLE NOW

Past the Glad and Sunlit Season: Poems for Halloween
by K. A. Opperman / Illustrated by Dan Sauer

October Ghosts and Autumn Dreams: More Poems for Halloween
by K. A. Opperman / Illustrated by Dan Sauer

The Withering: Poems of Supernatural Horror
by Ashley Dioses / Illustrated by Mutartis Boswell

The Voice of the Burning House
by John Shirley / Illustrated by Dan Sauer

The Ettinfell of Beacon Hill: Gothic Tales of Boston
by Adam Bolivar / Illustrated by Dan Sauer

Book of Shadows: Grim Tales and Gothic Fancies
by Manuel Arenas / Illustrated by Dan Sauer

The Miskatonic University Spiritualism Club
by Peter Rawlik / Illustrated by Dan Sauer

The Eldritch Equations and Other Investigations
by Peter Rawlik

Really, Really, Really, Really Weird Stories
(A New Edition with Four New Stories) by John Shirley

Not a Princess, but (Yes) There Was a Pea and
Other Fairy Tales to Foment Revolution
by Rebecca Buchanan

Halloween Hearts
by Adele Gardner

COMING IN 2023

Darker Than Weird: Fourteen Tales of Horror
by John R. Fultz

www.JackanapesPress.com
www.facebook.com/Jackanapes-Press

I AWAKEN IN OCTOBER

POEMS OF FOLK HORROR AND HALLOWEEN

SCOTT J. COUTURIER

FOREWORD BY REBECCA BUCHANAN
ILLUSTRATED BY DAN SAUER

"The Gods Came In Autumn" was originally published in *The Literary Hatchet* #23, 2019
"I Awaken In October" was originally published in *Spectral Realms* #15, 2021
"The Pumpkin Sprite" was originally published in *Eternal Haunted Summer* Winter Solstice issue, 2020
"Lord of Pumpkins" was originally published in *Spectral Realms* #10, 2019
"Autumn Sunflower" was originally published in *The Literary Hatchet* #25, 2020
"Darkness Dawns" was originally published in *The Literary Hatchet* #25, 2020
"All Fires Light The Wicker Man" was originally published in *Spectral Realms* #16, 2022
"Green Fever" was originally published in *Sanitarium Magazine* #3, 2020
"Winter's Grip" was originally published in *Eternal Haunted Summer* Winter Solstice issue, 2018
"Yule-Telling" was originally published in *Eternal Haunted Summer* Winter Solstice issue, 2017
"Year's Walk" was originally published in *Eternal Haunted Summer* Winter Solstice issue, 2021
"Shade-Bitten" was originally published in *The Audient Void* #3, 2017
"The Pixie-Ring" was originally published in *Spectral Realms* #16, 2022
"Forebear of the Stones" was originally published in *Eternal Haunted Summer* Winter Solstice issue, 2019
"Old Year's Night" was originally published in *Eternal Haunted Summer* Summer Solstice issue, 2020
"Planting Instructions" was originally published in *The Sirens Call eZine* #58, 2022
"Zephyr's Allure" was originally published in *Spectral Realms* #17, 2022
"Queen of Bees" was originally published in *The Fifth Di...* June issue, 2022
"Azazel-Pomps" was originally published in *The Fifth Di...* June issue, 2022
"Gray Grimalkin" was originally published in *Spectral Realms* #16, 2022
"Zephyr's Fair Child" was originally published by *Cosmic Roots and Eldritch Shores*, 2020
"When Black Tom Came" was originally published in *Spectral Realms* #9, 2018
"The Nachzehrer" was originally published in *Spectral Realms* #17, 2022
"Algol's Lamp" was originally published in *Eternal Haunted Summer* Summer Solstice issue, 2019
"Forbidden Fruit" was originally published in *Spectral Realms* #10, 2019
"September's Specter" was originally published in *The Literary Hatchet* #23, 2019

I Awaken in October: Poems of Folk Horror and Halloween

www.JackanapesPress.com

Cover and interior design by Dan Sauer
www.DanSauerDesign.com

First Paperback Edition

1 3 5 7 9 8 6 4 2

ISBN: 978-1-956702-09-5

For Grandma:
Thank you for listening.

Dear Heather &
Duncan,

Happy October!

Contents

Part 3 – Winter's Bite

Part 4 – The Witching Hour

ART 5 — A CROWN OF SEASONS

ILLUSTRATIONS

FOREWORD

I was first introduced to Scott J. Couturier's work when he submitted his poem "Yule-Telling" to my zine, *Eternal Haunted Summer*. It was dark and sensual and sensuous. Reading his poem was like falling into a Gothic novel, all velvet and shadows and crystal goblets of thick red wine.

This atmosphere of dread and desire persists through the body of his work. Firmly grounded in the world, in the change of the seasons and the passage of sun and moon, his poetry reminds us that we are *of* this world; that we exist as part of a larger cyclic ecosystem of flowers and fauns and fields of whispering grain.

Yet there is also a deep craving at the heart of his poetry, a hunger for awe and fear, an ache for wonder and danger. In Couturier's work, the flowers may be so vibrant because they are fed by bones and blood, the fauns have sharp teeth, and the grain whispers secrets not meant for human minds.

Such threads of awe and dread bind together this collection. Equal parts celebration, evocation, invocation, and incantation, these poems are a voluptuous immersion in the glories of autumn, the haunted forests of a pagan night, the marrow-deep chill of Yule, and the alchemical dance of the witch's hour. *I Awaken in October* is luxuriant, sumptuous, and exuberantly eerie: You will stand in awe before the Lord of Pumpkins and the Forest King, kneel in amazement at the humble majesty of daisies and redbreasted robins, and shiver in apprehension before Krampus and Old Black Shuck.

It was a pleasure losing myself inside these haunted pages, and I look forward—with some trepidation—to doing so again. Now, reader, it's your turn.

— Rebecca Buchanan
July 4th, 2022

INTRODUCTION

Autumn exerts a lover's hold over me. I savor the bright leaves and harvest customs that accompany the dying year; among my earliest sense-memories is the scent of the inside of a new-fashioned jack-o'-lantern, the candle just lighted. In spring's first incipient bud I see a sere crimson leaf, and every summer I wait with tremulous expectation, almost a reverent dread, for that first gust with a hint of cold (in northern Michigan it happens like clockwork on Lughnasadh or Lammas Day, August 1st).

As a kid, Halloween was my favorite holiday. Getting dressed up and venturing forth into the mysterious night exerted a strong fascination; it felt sacred and solemn, an echo of something beyond society's conscious recall. For one eve children *became* the monsters, knocking on strange doors to beg for candy, all while threatening a "trick" should the "treat" not be forthcoming. Flashes of glowing faces on porches—in kindergarten I was taught the legend of Stingy Jack, doomed to forever wander the earth with a carved turnip lit by hell's embers.

Later I would learn the history of Samhain, its origins and observances, and come to an understanding about my own worshipful relationship to the festival. It is the year's bier, crisply strewn with gold-and-red: the year's end for the ancient Celts. A time for phantoms to walk, for masks and mummery, for fortune-telling and invoked fright, when places are set at dinner for departed loved ones. A time for bonfires, witchcraft, and other elements of the "Old Ways," survivals of pagan practice from long before Christianity took root; a thinning of this reality's tenuous veil.

In *I Awaken In October* there are reflections of all four seasons, as well as verses in tribute to nature, horror and folkloric poems, poems of a spectral kind (the *super*natural), poems in praise of sun and moon, stars and earth. All, to me, form an ineluctable web: the power of nature expressed in literal and figurative guises, the realm of Faerie invoked, the "green fuse" (as Dylan Thomas called it) lit. Yet, everything hinges like a coffin's creaking lid on the Autumnal time of gloom and reflection, of somber rains and rites, gray days illuminated by ghosts of brilliant, swirling leaves. Autumn creates a temple for me, a sense of the numinous: it is the time of bringing in, which brings us, in turn, closer to our environment.

To honor one's place in the Year's Wheel, to live with the world as if it were sacred (it is), to merge with nature rather than technology: to honor and evoke the dead. There are many intentions in this collection, all suffused by a longing wistful and poignant—to awaken once more in October, when the foliage for one brief month matches my spirit.

—Scott J. Couturier
August 2, 2022

Part I

Autumn's Bier

The Gods Came in Autumn

The Gods came in Autumn:
borne on the ebbing season's
bier.
They filled the leaf-crowned wind
with wild songs, beyond reason:
drear
skies reeled to gold beneath their
gaze, leaves rushing to anoint
their faces, swarms of red-&-gold
brilliance.
The Gods' laughter was crisp &
sharp as a poniard's killing point:
in their mirthful wake crept cold.
Resilience
of life withered to pining seed as
harsher gods came, of Winter's breed.

I Awaken in October

I awaken in October,
just as gaunt ghost-tapers are lit:
I awaken in October as bat
& brume about chimney-hole flit.

I awaken in October
as sheaves shiver in evening's gloam;
I awaken in October as blue
moon's forebear rises, pale as bone.

I awaken in October,
from a September's restless sleep:
scent of decay's succor rises
from heaps of fiery leaves, mounded deep.

I awaken in October,
to a spirit's soft-speaking voice:
fae-folk fret 'mid the clover
as ruddy Jack-o'-Lanterns rejoice.

I awaken in October,
as from some dim-remembered dream—
all shores foreign save this strand
from whence witch-fires lurid gleam.

I awaken in October,
not once or twice, but thrice—
ghosts stalk the waning grain-stubble
docking tails from all the mice.

I awaken in October,
& fear now to sleep again,
lest this far & fair country should
fade, leaving only November's pain.

I awaken in October,
sworn to season's mystic writ—
I awaken in October, ah!
the enchantment & devout Mystery of it.

The Pumpkin Sprite

Pumpkin sprite alighting from gourd to gourd:
beneath Autumn's amethyst moon grown huge
she plumpens up pulp & swells seeds in horde,
subtle spirit of season's subterfuge.
For comes soon a boreal howl of winds,
corn shorn to bare stubble, grain threshed from stalk—
pumpkins flush ember-hued each fulsome rind
as fair Fall turns, key to bleak Winter's lock.
Yet—she flutters careless on vesperal airs,
all unseen save from vision's utmost edge:
kissing each of her orange charges with care,
dreaming away long gold days 'mid the sedge.

Vining coils entwine to caress her pale skin:
lamenting her wail when harvest-time begins,
trembling fey of delight, offspring of Gwyn—
night aglow with her children's carven grins.

Lord of Pumpkins

For K. A. Opperman

Into the patch I gleefully go,
to fix my roots, to coil & grow.

Lord of Pumpkins, once Man I was:
now, the omnipresent insect buzz
o'er luxuriant vines is dearly mine.
Through grass my greening tendrils twine.

Into the patch I gleefully go,
to fix my roots, to coil & grow.

Once Man, now vegetable I am.
But more: a Lord of Fields I am.
Of rot & mold & loamy wind
& the oatmeal-chest o'er-brimmed—
I am husk-rustle of each elfin leaf
as chill wind strikes at bowers brief.

Into the patch I gleefully go,
to fix my roots, to coil & grow.

The Dead all know me by my Name—
they dance 'round me a circle game.
Yet, hollow my flesh & put a candle in
& they flee exalting from my grin!
A hallowed god of olden Ways—
the squeal of sawing fiddle plays
as scythes dissever old Barley John:
the Season's come, & the Season's gone.

Into the patch I gleefully go,
to fix my roots, to coil & grow.

Once Man, my flesh was coarse to me.
A means to shed it sought I endlessly.
Fruitless quest, 'til Pan's luscious lute
summoned me forth to *become* Fruit.
Now splay I gloating in Summer's heat
as Autumn creeps nigh on stealthy feet:
below, the dead twitch impatient bones.
The skewed bulks of worn gravestones
lie heavy on each unsettled wight
yearning year-round for that Night of nights.

Into the patch I gleefully go,
to fix my roots, to coil & grow.

Lord of Pumpkins, once Man was I:
But no more Man. Pumpkin am I.

Autumn Sunflower

Thy head nods wisely in Autumn's cruel wind:
petals flare in gently unfolding foil.
To cloud-clad sun thy brilliant stare is blind—
chill rains fall, mocking thy untimely toil.
Yet—yellow as Summertide's choicest ray,
concentric spiral of seeds in situ,
bud-brooch upon cloak of Stygian gray.
Thy mere sight virtue of sunbeam imbues.
Art thou some sidereal star, void-lost,
searing 'cross space's stern infinitude?
Ageless light, with life-giving warmth embossed—
to fairer suns thou bear similitude.

Meanwhile, our native sun hides in disgrace:
jealous of its glory fixed on thy face.

At Summer's End

Summer's end comes austere, unlooked-for—
blight among the lote, pale blossoms
showing corpse pallors in ever-latening
dawn.

Creeping on golden rays that lengthen
spear-like, impaling the ailing year,
blossoms dozy with luscious droop,
lawns

parched in places to pates of bare earth,
decay already evident in hedge's train,
withered seed-pods blown on cooling
wind:

loath to rescind Life's sweet dominion,
yet wan & wanton for October's kiss,
lips of blissful greenery by desire
brimmed.

Cicadas haunt humid shadows, arid ray
of midday dimming behind oak boughs,
twilight lurking in bowers where roses
twine.

Geese arrow in flight, clouds of onion-husk
obscuring sun's swiftened descent,
clammy coat of dew as pumpkin swells on
vine.

August air succulent with harvest scent,
hanks of torn spiderweb ensnaring day,
moonlight blue & cool on paths that
wend

towards some unknown & mystic bend,
haunted by Autumn's creeping sway—
the ripened grape pends like a period
at Summer's end.

Autumn's Glory

Autumn's glory crowned by serest decay:
crimson-lit leaves rustle with weariness,
light dimming as night overtakes fair day.
Fires burn dimly, devoid of cheeriness.
Twilight's veiled moon a baleful lantern lit,
casting beams coldly on moss-mantled stones
engraved with eulogies by grievers writ,
demarcating dreamless domain of bones.
Yet—in loam-laden gust of Autumn's breath
these dead entrust per whispers that quaver
dread secrets of Life (& its fell mate, Death).
Amid the sedge, one brief red leaf wavers.

Autumn's glory globes all in crowning red:
Then chop! as Winter claims its regal head.

Autumn Come Knocking

Autumn come knocking—
acorns fall to crack & clatter,
rattle-tat-tatter in gloaming
evening's light.
Last cicada's expiring buzz—
leaves in muzzled majesty droop,
flowers dappled with darkling clots,
each yield-bowed stem askew
with weight of waxing nights.

Autumn come knocking—
fire inflaming crowns of green,
course of sap running cold
as squirrel & chipmunk wage war
to store up hoarded glean.
Faded heat wraith-like lingers,
wind from the north bold
& strange, rapping with brumal knuckle
on our wilting brains.

Autumn come knocking—
clatter-crash in underbrush,
drumming of nut-husk on roof.
Stag's antlers spread as frost
foliates the blossom's browning edge,
chimes tattling to telling breezes
of summer's drowse, now decayed by
long languishment & bitter freeze.
Nymphs huddle & mutter in the hedge.

Autumn come knocking—
veils of corpse-raiment cloud drift
& spatter earth with chill rains.
Sunlight pales from hale to dim:
vesperal spirits stalk from beyond life's rim
to lurk in turnrows scarred by plow.
Clip-clop—the headless horseman's ride
sounds on rime-slickened cement.
Hunter's moon rises, full & fell,
a wan & baleful revenant.

Autumn come knocking—
loud thump from beneath coffin's lid.
Fatted pumpkins brood in shade,
awaiting that eve when spirits bid
all veils be rent in riotous twain.
Elves raid the wheat-stocked wains
as scarecrows stalk with sickle blades,
summer's death a sudden shock,
murder of croaking crows in flock.
Dusk's insect murmur, like an echo, fades.

Embalm Me in Autumn

Embalm me in Autumn,
beneath an orange Harvest Moon,
Summer's waning fraught
by season's impinging gloom,
all Beauty of life's bounty
ebbing with elegance of a swoon:

Embalm me in Autumn,
slathered in cadaverous leaves
like ground & grave alike.
See! Before me bows to grieve
a ghast of Winter's shade,
sorrowing as warm days yet deceive:

Embalm me in Autumn,
pricks & poniards of crimson
crowning boughs of green,
herbage already reeking brown
& cold rains roiling steady,
skies with woolen wracks all glum:

Embalm me in Autumn,
drowsy with September's dream,
mushroom-caps clammy
poking from my soggy seams,
snails slithering to numb
my tongue, devour my screams:

Embalm me in Autumn,
each day eager pared in breadth,
waxing night a wonder
as ages bygone upstir from death,
ghosts roaming roads
& livid firmament's fervid depth:

Embalm me in Autumn,
to a harpsichord's jangling tune,
tied tight with cobwebs
& bindings from a mummy hewn,
ghouls attending where I lie
to ensure my bier is crimson-strewn—
beneath a weird & woeful sky
lit by a leering Harvest Moon.

PART 2

NATURE'S BOWER

Darkness Dawns

It is nigh.
The wind is high—
sunset red in sky bathes
the orange groves in garish light.
Beyond, a veil of blade-thin night
draws up from far firmament's scrim
to dog him—fair Sun—to dim antipodes.
A delicious chill of evening kisses us
as scarabs from arid dust-girt lands
alight upon our hands & brows,
iridescent in sunset's death:
night dawns now, & every
sweetly forbidden
thing allows.

DVS ©2022

All Fires Light the Wicker Man

All fires light the Wicker Man—
burn higher, higher, as we sing this song!
Morris dancers mark the tune,
praising Sun & praising Moon,
hobby-horse hungry for virginity
as we raise worship to our trinity:
for the Goddess of the Orchards
& the grim God of the Waves,
& last the Summer's searing sun,
day-bright beacon of divinity.

All fires light the Wicker Man—
burn higher, higher, as we sing this song!
Within, a sacrifice writhes & screams,
even as the brass band blares
& mad hares in dozens break the seams
of Winter-cold earth beneath our feet!
The frame goes up in startling flame,
roasting alive our offered game
beside a heathen Christian's life.
Hey, ho, cups full to utmost brim!
All hail coming of May's Queen!

All fires light the Wicker Man—
burn higher, higher, as we sing this song!
The shepherd's servant bawling prayers
as we fall to revelry in throng,
crazed rutting midst the ash & blood,
clad only in coiling crowns of furze
as Summer's first lust is slaked.
The sun sets as the Wicker Man's head
falls inward with a roaring flood
of flame: the heretic (still alive!)
for a final time wails out Christ's name.

All fires light the Wicker Man—
burn higher, higher, as we sing this song!
Let the harvest be plentiful, & the Summer long!

Daisies

Daisies in lazy profusion lay strewn
'neath unfurling fiddlehead ferns in June.
Sun-glad eyelets of yellow show brazen,
samite petals white with Summer's blazon:
though immortal-seeming, gone all too soon.

Come further flowers to color the plot—
amber hues, blue dusk of forget-me-not.
Honeysuckle seeps scent to clement winds
as lilacs their briefest beauty rescind.
Vines twine upwards in effusion from rot.

Yet—daisies' reign set in forested glens:
on their fidelity the bee depends.
Busy mummery, blossom to blossom,
pollen-clad as a priestess-queen awesome
dons robes: dais & throne each bloom attended,
brows dusted in gold precious beyond sum.

Daisies deign their benign vigil to maintain
'till Autumn unwinds its funereal train:
then wither!, awaiting Spring's succulent rain
& new thralls to renew old worship again,
hierophantic plant in mysterium crowned.

The Forest King

The Forest King uplifts his brow—
rises from early evening's gloaming.
Tree limbs stir as a lowing cow
calls from her too-late a-roaming.

Lanterns glisten 'cross gilded fields
where wheat stands rampant, phallic-bold—
drowsy breezes caress their yield
of fructifying kernels, greening to gold.

The Forest King draws savory breath
of seed & spore & pollen grain,
uplifting himself from loaming earth
to walk by night, all Nature his fane.

Now too-tired sun is setting, gone—
now twilight things set up their chatter.
Toads chirrup from farmhouse lawns,
or banter in deep tarns of toadly matters.

Spirits stir, stride sky & land ascendant—
The Forest King exhales his breath.
Moon's gleam mimes an opaline pendant,
presiding virgin-wan over solar death.

A greening creeps into fulsome soil—
breath of flower & bee, bulb & tree.
Ghosts walk old roads home from toil
done in some other, archaic century.

Now, chickens are all fast asleep—
now a hiss of night wind on leaves.
Back to his hold the Forest King creeps
as fae-folk flock to dreamers' eaves.

Then—the long, cool, all-presiding night.
Stars flicker brightly, emissaries of light.
The Forest King reassumes his throne—
inhales deeply seeds to be tomorrow blown.

Pan

What of the groves?
What of the hour?
What walks the night with power?

Obscur'd the moon
by his high horns—
the mountain-loping
Pan strides with witches
in their swarms.

What of fires on hilltops?
What of revelry & wine?
What of stars bawdy in firmament's bower?

IAO Pan! Hooves send thunder—
piping madly notes of passion
from his priapic reeds.
Red moon rent asunder as
groves burn, heatless with flame.
Scent of loins, wet goat fur,
bray of lust on balmy winnow.

What of misery's weary cycles?
What of Humanity's self-extirpation?
What worries a dead world, drearily husked?

The grapes burst full yet—
old skins for the oldest wine.
Pan laughs amid melting tundra
& withering bough,
mind obscene with new designs.

Robin Redbreast

Robin Redbreast—your august April
arrival declares Spring's ardent turning.
A-hop to hunt among leafy beds,
crimson crest fat, fulgent & burning—
above, sun ascendant beams
rays to waken life's somnolent yearning.
Peck-&-prance—a thick worm writhes
in your beak, loaming's savory tithe.
Above, blithe chickadees weave orbicular
in flight by spiderling's nascent lace.
Green spears stab upwards from earth,
encroaching at an invader's pace—
smallest florets flourish in sedge
as squabbling squirrels nourish themselves
on bounty of overstocked stores,
Winter a pale wraith Spring's bold sprite
takes delight in spurning. Sage & ivy
emerge from hoar-clad repose: hares hurry
behind their own racing shadows.
Soon, bluebells will blossom & toll,
mayflies emerge, & mosquitoes in swarm
seek out their sanguinary goal.
A hot season of languid work & rest—
to all this, Robin Redbreast, you attest
in futures soon-to-be. Yet now, April
still stings with nightly frosts: buds cringe,
stymied back to buck-brown nubs.

Away, Robin, to your obscure nest,
nursing eggs of Summer's incipience;
Phoenix of ever-lengthening day,
of your carol we but reverent recipients.

Hymn to Sunlight

Greatest Divine Sunlight!
Holistic light of unbroken day!
You flow in rivers to gild bright
corn-in-shuck, golden vibrant hay.
Drowse of insects a crown—
hallowed halo with humming rife,
inciting life amid withered
remnants of winter's strife.
Unbroken your ray as it arrays
verdure in verdancy's sheen:
tomatoes ripen as fragrance fey
of heaths, whose florets dapple green,
upon the nostrils taunting play.

Sunlight—incantations to Night
cannot blunt your blazing sway.
Sear away dusk-hued heights
heralding end of your endless day!—
stars erupt to envy your might.
You depart: but not in flight.

Hymn to Nature

The earth a trembling lover
breathless before night's fall:
leaves laughing paganly
in will-o'-the-wisps of wind.
Sweet night's balm brings
crickets to merry song,
moon a marble tomb
barren of inscription:
toads mutter in mad throng,
summoning to sanctuary
the old soul's lamentation.
Nature, purest mistress,
fertile Maiden, mercurial Mother,
& crow-winged Crone:
your breath of tomorrows
is blown ecstatic,
breeze fruitful with grain,
a moan of feral pleasure
ebbing upwards from loam.
To die. Can it be so terrible?
Just the body returning home.

Night Trembles

The stars do cry a solemn song
at incipience of stirring dawn.
The nightingale may piping cry
as sun's blushing suffuses sky—
to wooded deeps retreats the faun,
dew dazzling on nightshade's lawn,
oozing ointments which make witches fly.
Night trembles, tarries lover-like, is gone.

Part 3

Winter's Bite

Green Fever

Itching at his wrist, the
gardener grows anxious.
Outside falls snow: Winter is
come to claim its throne, &
all verdure vanquish.

The itch intensifies. Still,
the snow: an urge to plant,
to see things grow, wracks
the gardener's greening brain.
He begins to pant.

Scabrous growths mar
his forearms: patches of mold.
Without, the fallow earth,
barbed by mockery of stubble,
languishes in cold.

The long, long Winter:
it stretches from November
to frost-fraught April.
His eyelids twitch, his
fingers convulse: remember

the delicious new sprouts
of darling May waxing to
fulgence, fruit swollen on vine,
the pollen-laden kiss of wind
that perishes at Winter's rue.

The growth is spreading.
In his brain blades of green
sprout from gray matter,
piercing a pate laved in
verdurous sweat-sheen.

Roots elongate from fingers,
distend achingly from unclad soles.
Now, a blizzard bares razor-white
teeth: all life devoured, reduced
to guttering coals.

& the months ahead: the black,
verglas-glazed elder night!
His fever intensifies: he radiates
like compost, digesting himself
to off-stave the blight.

The green sweat gathers into
a nurturant pool: roots displace
floorboards in quest for soil.
The gardener chokes as florets unfurl
from mouth & ear & face.

It is May: long has he been ill
with the green fuse's burning.
Now, he moves as no plant
should move: aspect a-flower, body
to a tree bole turning.

The lust to sow, to grow:
it overcomes, transmuting blood
to sap. Fleshy branches burst
from his brain-pan: he surges
forth on loaming flood

to root himself in the garden
long-forlorn & Winter-scourged.
Creepers fix deep to artesian veins
as branches arc to trembling buds
with hot new life gorged.

***

The Tree: it was seen by
many, remarked upon for
its beauty & lush foliage.
In Summer its leaves flush
red, as if with gore.

In Autumn, they turn the
palest color of cold-bitten
flesh. It bears uncouth fruits: all
who taste of them are with a
wasting fever smitten.

Keep the Old Ways Close

Keep the Old Ways close—
keep the hearth-stone warm,
safe haven from storm's blister
& snowfall's brutal bite.

Bonfires crown hilltops far,
burning as a field of stars
fallen to Winter's bitter earth.
Orion rises, jubilant host!

Weave circles about the flame—
surrender that which is tame
to night-time's intoxicant spell,
transfixed by pagan rite—

ecstasies of soul & flesh,
writhing in heed sans shame
as loins ache with need to quell.
Above, Moon full as a boast,
brazen as an unblushing whore,
firmament & forest enmeshed—

Keep the Old Ways close.
Kindle anew, in Darkness, Light.
Raise in praise a hallowed toast
so our ailing Sun may be refreshed,
& know promise of May's Queen
while still by December's hoar
held thralled from sight, in dream.

Winter's Grip

I heard a baleful note of terror
on a mid-Winter's night:
peering up I saw the sky
suffused with a spectral light.
Sharp horn-blasts smote my ears,
a baying of many hounds:
turning, I began madly to run
towards a scope of sacred mounds.

Here were many warriors inhumed:
here elves were said to stealthy lurk.
Crouching down I concealed myself
amid midnight's deep & riming murk.
Above, the sky grew brighter yet:
I heard a thunder, as of horses.
The hoary moon was then outshone
by a spirit-throng in their courses.

A multitude eclipsed the sky:
gibbering, wailing, stampeding dead!
Fae nipped noxiously at their heels
& a horned hunter rode at their head.
Some goaded pale & faceless steeds:
others rode men, but were not men.
Crying out, I cast my face to earth
& strove to preserve my mortal ken.

Yet—I say it was not to be.
These silver hairs? I earned them well!
For holes yawned ope upon the mound
to spew forth hunters forsworn of Hel.
Clattering joints that were not mine
reached my horribly attuned ear:
corpses thrust up from the loam,
bones worm-flensed & winter-sere.

I felt a touch on my trembling palm—
the ice-brand of a dead man's grip
fumbled to clasp me, to draw me nigh:
with a wail I gnawed my nether lip.
The welling of hot & living blood
occluded the summons from the sky:
the touch withdrew, the hunters rode on,
leaving me alive yet yearning to die.

I know not how I survived that night:
does any fool know aught who has seen
Wotan masterly in black command
surge 'cross Yuletide's starry screen?
Nevermore do I venture near those mounds
when Winter's grip lies on the land:
lest I should hear a baying of hounds,
or the dead wrest anew my pining hand.

Yule-Telling

Inside this sacral fane the flame
burns in reverence to that night
which is omnipotent in Name;
it casts hallowed shadows to flight

yet sets them also to strident dance—
rituals deepen as Winter's cold
hurls forth its Hyperborean lance
to stimulate the life force, honeyed-gold.

Greetings are given, in bawdy tone—
drunken roars swell home & mead-hall,
inciting warmth to hoariest bone
afflicted by mortality's shading pall.

About the Yule-tree gathered in song—
hearthfires burn a sempiternal light
as dying year's specters & worried wrongs
dissolve into an atmosphere bedight.

Tales are then told, in whispered round;
Winter's shade cast in spectral guise.
Geists frighten in grim fables profound
as flame to moody ember dies.

Desecrated graves, & bodies cold
with Yuletide's preternatural bite
struggling up from snow-dappled mold
to haunt that gelid, crystalline night—

drifts of white obscure the tread
which marks no imprint on earthly things.
A sense of Winter's Promethean dread
gives to black fancy frost-fretted wings.

I shiver, & wonder at the ice-clad earth.
I contemplate those that slumber beneath.
Some loving semblance of heat-laced breath
I to them in these rude stanzas bequeath.

Krampusnacht is Coming

(inspired by the Alpine folk tradition of Krampus, an anthropomorphic goat/demon figure who punishes naughty children on the night of December 5th, known as Krampusnacht)

Krampusnacht is coming! Coming!
Birch-switches hiss on the midnight air!
Krampusnacht is coming! Coming!
Chains a-rattle! Brazen bells that blare!

On cold of December's bitterest rime
comes Krampus from the alpine heights—
his cloven hooves beat diabolic time as
he stalks the streets his namesake night.

Krampusnacht is coming! Coming!
Children shiver in their beds, affright!
Krampusnacht is coming! Coming!
Cold wraith-winds blow out the light!

There is no way to avoid his switch,
no escape from his black basket's weft.
Beware if you yield to mischief's itch,
for no brat can elude his judgment deft.

Krampusnacht is coming! Coming!
Lay out a saucer, offertory of schnapps!
Krampusnacht is coming! Coming!
He will be wroth should your tribute lapse!

Bearing bundles of coal & bloodied Ruten,
long tongue lolling with Winter's lust:
accompanied by goose-footed Perchten,
Krampus hauls off the wicked, ivy-trussed.

Krampusnacht is coming! Coming!
No bells of Christendom can off-ward him!
Krampusnacht is coming! Coming!
Wailing bulges flail at his black sack's scrim!

Form of a devil, but far far older—
Echo of the Horned One, scion of Pan.
If you've been bad, peer over your shoulder
when nights of December roll round again.

For—
Krampusnacht is coming! Coming!

For December

Such drear weather sere spirits must impose.
Cold coils on one's breath in serpents of rime,
sunlight a fitful friend, oft prone to doze.
Snowflakes measure out the meter of Time,
stubble strewing fields with phalli of blight,
each gust the respire of a malign clime.
Long & bleak stretches each frost-weary night,
a prisoner wracked for some obscure crime;
the forest conspires with clattering limbs,
winds wailing concatenation of hymns
as banks of intruding white start to climb—

December: your touch tarnishes my soul,
forebear of darkness & feaster of coal.

The Frost-Wight

A claw-like scritching sounds on yonder door,
talons trailing o'er panes by frost obscured.
Winds moan wickedly wroth from off the moor—
in despite, I sense myself sore allured.
Pining to admit some phantom of snows,
or fling windows wide to greet northern night
in whatever embodiment it knows:
sensual these stirrings stemming from fright!
Now, about my bright chimney-hole it flies
on cold wings older than sun can reckon,
filling wastelands wide with its eerie cries—
a wail to repel, but also beckon.

Madness it must seem to any who read—
how I fled into night, my soul new-freed,
eager to feed that wight's ravenous need.

Winter's Wrath

Tumultuous medium of tempests,
eternal vault of chill void-veiling blue—
your bale the last wraithlike leaf freely wrests,
attesting to all your bitterness slew.
Gales of gloaming snow borne on night's ascent,
dervishes of devilish cold that coat
the black corpse of Summer, beneficent;
crystals entomb toadstools of grotesque bloat.
The wind! A carving-knife of icy edge
to incise heartstrings & marbleize breath,
each bleak blast renewing a dire wolf's pledge
to Death's stark ideal in icicles wept.

Winter's wrath stalks abroad, hunger unchained:
gusts festered by ghosts of those it has slain.

Year's Walk

(inspired by the Swedish divinatory practice of Årsgång)

Abide in darkness all the day before.
Take care to cast eye upon no open flame.
No food or drink, nor spoken word
must pass lips that would later prophesy.

An evening's stroll for prognostication—
chill the weather, fat snow-flakes falling,
barren wind & wolves' howl haunting
waiting night. What will be encountered
as this Year dies, as moon's dim light
permeates unclean, restless clouds—as
ice thickens & boreal vapors rise?
To show any sign of fright will foil one's
quest; to laugh or even smile, to exchange
word, or take any along beside you. If
you meet another on your way, together
may you proceed, but should either speak—
dire reprisals must you equally reap.

Crisp crunch of snow underfoot: faint
things scuttle at edges of vision, trees
girt with mail of adamant white. Weird
winds gust about, animating flakes into
spectral forms: to these one must pay no
heed. A steady step, heart beating even—
resist wayward urge to whistle as mists
of cloying cold coil about in ghostly
cloister. Things howl in near-distance that
no one can name—deeper, deeper
into that primal wood, far from any fair

fire or companion, where the hoar-cold
is bitterest, there to walk & witness the
pale auguries as they parade on past.

A funeral carriage, drawn by headless
horses: the body inside is well-known.
A death omen, to be borne back to
town & somberly conferred. Onwards,
towards the too-distant churchyard of
St. Stephens: will-o'-wisps pulse in dull
array, away over frozen swampland where
no life stirs. What does stir—abyssal
spirits from days of old, Winter geists
& brook-horses stretched long as
Midgard's serpent, bearing trains of
wailing children to grisly drowning ends.
One's step must not falter, whatever
horrible visage leers from the trees:
huldra-nymphs wracked with lust &
hunger, looking for meal or mate to steal.

Further on, & fresh visions arise—
a fertile harvest, yes, a bountiful year
unmarked by famine, plague, or war.
A good year, save for those who will die—
but, a good year to die in. One runs risk
of seeing oneself drawn along in phantasmal
hearse: hasten to the sought churchyard,
ignoring half-icy streams that run blood-
red with wine. Fruity scent of faerie vintage

tingles the nose as grave-stones hove into sight:
absurdity tempts too, trio of flatulent mice
drawing a square-wheeled wain, owl droppings
plopping on shoulders, tempting laugh
or curse. Once on church grounds, fresh
graves are seen dug amid the snow: stones
spell out names of five more dead.
Psalms chant up from each coffin-bed,
soil roiled by mortal sinners disinterred—
from the church comes a noisome stirring,
something profane taking place in the nave.

Three quick circuits, counter-clockwise. An
eye to the keyhole, & blow—what horror
or wonder is then beheld! More than one walker
returns sans an eye: others are struck blind,
dumb, or mad. Some vanish, provender
or partner for wily wood-wives; some wander
lost into icy mires, lured by puckish lights.
To reach that keyhole & peer through at the
Old Year writhing on Christ's altar, sacrifice
to pitiless Time, bane & master of all gods:
dead masses gathered in throng to witness
& worship, phantom limbs upraised in praise.
Alas, what auguries come during the awful
Year's Walk! As sun dawns the seer stumbles
back home to waiting kin, ripened with oracles,
haunted & harrowed, oft evermore queer.

Part 4

The Witching Hour

Shade-Bitten

A Poem for Samhain

The flame within the pumpkin glows
a rich & ruddy light;
without, the season immemorially flows
towards the Memnons of the Night.
A frigid chill infests the bones
& strips verdure from elder trees,
whilst the Earth seeks darkling repose
from Summer's sweet, burning disease.
Inwards curl the lingering buds
embalmed in armature of frost;
the earth turns to world-wearied mud
& the mind to things wicked, wild & lost.

Then, in a whisper of errant wind,
one may hear the chattering of the dead;
their speech no oblivion can rescind
& living blood is their sacral bread.
One night only, on Dear Samhain,
they creep forth from tumulus & howe,
hungry for mortal blood & brains
& all else Death's bourne would disallow.

Nature! Kindest in impartial plod—
Only on Samhain can the weighty sod
part to admit undead remains.
Otherwise, proud Nature disdains
to allow such spurious reanimation,
Mould being the seat of all creation.

Yet—once a year the restless wights
reinhabit their lineaments of yore,
& seek remembrance of earthly delights
via copious consumption of human gore.
Thus, I keep a warding pumpkin lit
on my stoop throughout this sacral Eve,
lest I should become shade-bit
or my guts some ghoulish hunger relieve.

Old Black Shuck

Some still pray (so they say) to Old Black Shuck.
Especially by twilight, traveling the roadway—
better to appease than confront his balefire stare,
or see the waring bristle of his ebony hair.

Faithful hound of Jack o' the Lantern, he howls
as he roams heath & highway, phantom jowls
bright with teeth whetted on St. Elmo's fire:
to behold him by night betokens prophecy dire.

My uncle, he saw Old Black Shuck (he did!)
Of every tooth his poor head soon was rid,
gnashing away in the deeps of his sleep
like a ravenous dog with hot flesh in its keep.

My nephew, I aver he beheld the Black Hound:
ever since he shies from all harsh sight & sound.
His father, he saw that damnable thing too:
dead in two years, rent & emptied of grue.

My wife, she glimpsed his furnace-red eyes
one winter's night: still lamentation she cries.
Our child, born dead within three weeks' time:
slain by hoarfrost, blue limbs bound in rime.

Me, once bandits beset me, stove in my head,
stole all my belongings & left me for dead.
Staggering aimless, I caught his infernal glare—
yet home safely he led me, demanding no fare.

Mangy ghost-mongrel of moorland & path,
will you allot aid or bestow spectral wrath?
Your wail, honed as fang of December's gale—
your bite like icicles: bramble-tangled your tail.

Horrid huge head, foaming maw, then disappear!
Stench of wet fur & offal lingers everywhere,
though no paw print marks the stony ground:
in near distance bays & hunting-horns sound.

Old Black Shuck (they say) still roams abroad,
leaving some dead, some a-feared, others awed.
Should he guide you aright or to doom, all who see
him tremble as they recall the same dread memory.

The Pixie-Ring

Ring of mushrooms by the wayside—
what within your fey perimeter abides?
A shiver of silvern bells at dusk
sounds as evening exhales its musk:
orbs on the dark garth swarm & glide.

Ring of mushrooms, mottled red in hue—
who tempts your periphery will Faery rue.
Perilous Realm lures down uncanny trails,
seducing hapless hikers beyond the veil
of tableaux which mortal ken must eschew.

Above, sere oak leaves of umber cast
rattle like rotted teeth, fair Summer past.
Fungi flourish in hoary dales of gloom,
pale caps clammy with November's doom—
the pixie-ring is wilted, with blight aghast.

Perish back to the pitch-black loaming,
gateway sealed by Autumn's gloaming!
Elfin songs grow strained as first snow falls,
retreating to fabulous jewel-fret halls
where the enrapt revel, faery-ales foaming.

Forebear of the Stones

(inspired by the practices of Ár nDraíocht Féin)

Hands raised, he opens the Gates—
invoking Odin, Dagda, Freya, Hecate
in sonorous address.
The silver cup his well—
World-Tree signified by
a sturdy oak with sere red leaves.
Forebear of the Stones,
sinews lit by mead's inspiration,
he appeases the Outdwellers:
Let us be.
Offerings cast into flame,
songs sung & runes consulted,
Spirits of Land & Ancestor
given reverent fee.
Tonight is Samhain:
moon a crooked scythe
of silver dissevering stars.
Morrigan! Eater of the dead!
Tonight your crows haunt
the heart of all necropoli.
The ritual is completed, but
the Gates are not shut,
provender instead laid out—
wine, fruit, meat, bread—
to satiate any attendant dead.
The druids bow low communal head,
speak words of remembrance
for those dearly loved & lost,
their ghosts abroad this one eve to tread.

Shining Ones, look with favor upon
those who practice the Old Ways on
Samhain night—
descendants of oak & ash, ivy & holly,
of menhir, barrow, & woad-blued clay.
So these ancient practices are kept:
even now, even today.

Old Year's Night

(inspired by the folk traditions of Tristan da Cunha, world's most isolated inhabited island)

The Okalolies are out tonight—
Romp-a-stomp, chomp-a-glomp!
Seeking stray waifs to marmalise,
as the Old Year dies they stir & rise.

Women they yearn to flush with fright—
Howl-a-growl, foul-a-scowl!
At twilight they prowl the village lanes—
peering in windows, scratching at panes.

Daemonic visages of wightish might—
Glare-a-ware, tooth-a-bare!
They stalk the night with burning stares,
horns up-thrust from goatish hair.

Beware brutish knockings at the door—
Thump-a-glump, rump-a-wump!
Answer not, lest your supper's repast
go to glut the gut of each eager ghast.

The Okalolies are out tonight—
Crack-a-whack, hack-a-thwack!
They relish each poppet's puny scream,
topple the cattle & curdle the cream.

Your potato patch they'll strike with blight—
Hob-a-nob, mob-a-bob!
They'll flay your thatch, bite your boarder:
mischief the evening's infernal order.

Only at midnight may it be put right:
Bell-a-knell, fell-a-spell!
The fishing gong is madly rung—
again & again the hammer swung.

Cries are raised to New Years bright—
Ring-a-ding, sing-a-ling!
The savor of braais floods the air
as kegs are broached & bonfires flare.

The Okalolies are out tonight—
Haunt-a-flaunt, chaunt-a-gaunt!
Having wrought their wicked wrack
on midnight's blast they cackle back
to deep sea-graves, abyssal black—

Old Year, put out the light!

Autumn's Imp

Amongst boughs of ocher & fire-red
he weaves & dances, nods his head:
singing songs of incipient frost,
Autumn's Imp honors all the lost
souls abroad in search of old homestead.

He cackles with glee at northerly gales,
tap-dances in time with threshing flails—
pasting bright leaves to cheek & brow
Autumn's Imp capers with a ribald sow
beneath Hunter's Moon by fell mists veiled.

As tree limbs strip to nakedness barren,
off come his lendings of leaf & heron
feathers collected by salty marsh pools—
nude, unencumbered, All Hallows he rules,
Autumn's Imp Sabbat's adamant baron.

Psychopomp, he presides over passing year,
gnawing Time's bone through ghoul's grisly leer.
At first snowflake's fall he shivers & bays,
succumbing to Winter's delirious daze:
only next Autumn will the Imp again appear.

Planting Instructions

Cut hand, insert seed into palm.
Infuse incision with bloodmeal balm.
Keep fingers cupped, as if to hold
a sprout's incipient stem in mold.
Clod your palm with graveyard dirt
& feel the seedling start to spurt.
Eager roots pervade your veins
& viscera: this will cause pains.
Pain is requisite to prime the seed—
torment its chief nutritional need.

With that hand you must do awful things:
disembowel & brawl, peel off wings.
It must go black with sinning's stain
before your seed grows beyond a grain.
At last! the sprout will greening unfurl
from a sod-jet claw that cannot uncurl.
Fresh agonies as roots rapidly expand
far beyond five fingers & palm of hand:
threading arteries well-nigh your heart
fibers inundate, never to depart.

Finally, with fleeting conscious might
you dig a hole deep as your height
& one arm-span: you then climb down
& extend up the sprout's serrate crown.
Let tendrils germinate overnight—
come next morning's creeping light
they will rake all excess soil in
'till it fills your hole to loamy brim.
Planted so, you shall die & live anew:
such a bloom as in Lilith's Eden grew.

Zephyr's Allure

A lonely idyll beside the lake—
aspens droop in late August's daze as
cicadas trill for ailing Summer's sake,
sky shot with sun-ray's succulence.

I espy a quiver above the water—
shiver of ethereal forms in dance.
Maids of pollen-down, fey daughters
of Summer's subtly ebbing trance.

I watch as they trip over lily-pads,
vitalized by slow & solemn gusts
of fair season's ending, ever-sad:
leaves fleck the lake with flakes of rust.

I feel the reverie of a faerie-dream
overcome me as I observe their spell.
Perfumes from worlds beyond the seam
of waking life lure me to blissful dwell

in kingdoms wrought of airy space,
where cornices of scalloped cloud
array opaline palaces of an elder race,
courts where no human thing is allowed.

Except—when the invitation is given,
one may shed mortality's immodest guise
& from its ailments forever be riven,
a guest of Mab with dew-dazzled eyes.

My heart beats faster as they drift near,
fragrant breeze a kiss upon gaping lips.
Yet, I ken also the clammy kiss of fear
as I see grinning skulls girt at their hips.

Five maids in all, of susurrus & down,
whispering sweet tones of zephyr's allure.
I tremble as they raise up a woven crown
of reeds, reeking with rank air impure.

Only then does that fearsome drowse
of pixie-torpor strike from my limbs.
With a cry their coronation I disavow:
each skull wears a selfsame diadem!
Another woeful gust, & I am alone again.

Faunus Walks

Faunus walks the wild wood tonight—
sets my heart to fluttering fright.
His pipes heard at evening's gloaming,
out 'mongst glade & grove a-roaming,
eager for all to come & dance—
yearning to slake his livid lance.

On spring wind goaty essence gusts:
horned & virile, hungers robust,
he sets seed in both bull & cow,
& either maid or youth may vow
by his reeds, in sonorous lust.
They return grinning, drenched in musk.

I hear his hooves on mountain crag—
phallus bold, backlit by Moon's brag,
he capers to crotala clacked
by nymphs & fauns, all double-backed.
An orgy wrought of woodland's wine:
debauchery a trance Divine.

Some diviners do sleeping lie
'pon sacral goat hides, gramarye
sought within sylvan visions deep:
future's doom theirs to solemn reap.
Meantime dark clouds scud ruddy past
a moon of luscious sanguine cast,
dyed by blood of sacrifice massed.

Faunus walks the wild wood tonight,
drunk on revels by godly right.
Mid stands of black priapic stone,
feral he ruts & brays & moans—
succulence of his pleasures breed
this genesis of Nature's need,
sin no foul thing one must atone.

Queen of Bees

Garbed in golden flow of silks cloy-scented,
scepter dripping profuse with nectar's dew;
Her eyes black globes like jewels segmented,
her kisses fell stings, sought to lover's rue.
The Bee Queen reigns from her fractalline throne,
brow crowned in coronet of buzzing wings;
In flashes of cruelty her mirth is shown,
her favor envenomed—wroth pain it brings!
Secreting sweetness from her every pore,
a honey within heart's compartments made;
Swarm engirding her as their sacred store,
forsaking lion's corpse, by Samson slayed—
Carnate hive alive with insect furor!

Her comb of succulence a lure divine:
on those begging to taste she gloating dines
as in her breast another queen reclines.

Azazel-Pomps

Azazel-pomps in clumps profound
flourish 'mid this burial ground.
Demon blooms of acidic blue—
mere sight of their accursed hue
blinds eyes of both man & beast.
Below, their roots infernal feast
on interred souls, ages laid at rest:
grosser they grow. Each bud attests
to torments in the restive tomb,
coffins recast as racks of gloom.
Black creepers cruelly pry apart
unquiet dead in that loaming dark—
ghostly spores of an azure grue
rise to follow what ill winds blew,
eager to infest where the dead rest true.

Hexennacht

Witches gather
   in a glabrous glade—
beneath gravid moon
   fell offerings are made.

Hide of oxen,
   yet hot with blood—
Mandrake-root
   shrieking, wet with mud.
Skull of babe
   still-born to a whore—
bronze daggers
   black with archaic gore
slit baying gullet
   of a gorge-ball'd goat.
Heady essence flows
   in red arcs from its throat.

Round about
   the cromlech stones,
coven weaving
   a webbing of moans—
scarce garments
   ecstatically cast away
as the Sabbat-night
   waxes, fierce & fey.
Chanting rises,
   a wickedly mounting roil:
smoke & song ascend
   in cacodemon's coil!

More offerings
made as night wears old.
From saint's tomb
a clipping of corruptious mold.
Sacral sapphires
lunar-girt, olibanum from a mummy's lung—
Witch-rood bent
in a hoop, heaps of pestilent leper's dung.
Hensbane, holly,
ash-sprig & dead man's clay—
at ritual's heart
leers a tumid, Pan-like baphomet.

Finally, a
human sacrifice is burned,
from still-hot
ashes umbral oracles discerned.
The moon above
grows sanguine-flushed
as if with blood
its cadaveric cheeks were blushed.
Cruor & wine
are combined, imbibed—
golden copulations
nullity of flesh circumscribe.

Then—away!
on wings of pitch-black astral shroud.
May's sun rises redly,
stained by seer-pyre's smolderous cloud.

Gray Grimalkin

Gray grimalkin slinks & stalks
as Jack his All Hallows round walks,
dispensing scares & sacred frights,
grin glowing in every pumpkin's light.

Gray grimalkin likes this night
best of all: shadow-realms her right,
she rubs on skewed cemetery stones,
welcoming witches with feral moans.

Gray grimalkin sees souls rise
unquiet from graves to starry skies;
swatting at each phantom's trail,
she runs to romp in ghost-lit dales.

Gray grimalkin preens & yowls,
purrs & hisses & exalting prowls,
teeth red-stained by graveyard rats,
gore of mice & ichor of bats:

Gray grimalkin on Hallowe'en!
The eve is yours, fell feline Queen.
Take your prey as specters shock,
goblins titter & Mab's train flocks.

Gray grimalkin on Hallowe'en!
Familiar of Scratch, sly & keen!
As dawn's ray peeps she falls asleep,
reliving it all in slumbers deep.

Zephyr's Fair Child

Fickle sprite of middle air: your blue hair
& azure eyes dazzle me to delight.
I spot the surplice of sunlight you wear,
sparkling as you spin in dizzying flight:
a crown of acorn for your elfin brow,
stout sword of thistle-sting strung at your side.
I see you strut upon a willow bough,
then—disappear! with effervescent glide.
Ever have I craved the Perilous Call,
hearkened for Mab's overture, stood in rings
of mushroom on eves when evil things crawl,
yet no sight have I had—save of your wings!

Fitful faerie of cloud, zephyr's fair child;
you vanish, but my soul remains beguiled.

Guests of October

Guests of October, lingering too long,
reluctantly melding with Autumn's loam.
Carven faces arrayed in rotting throng,
grinning out gayly 'mid November's gloam:
each decaying Jack filled by chilly rain
& massed corpses of fat & fallen flies,
crisp smiles ripened to grimaces of pain,
black mold glaring from behind incised eyes.
Guests of October, shining once so bright
to ward off spooks of ulterior spheres,
while welcoming trick-or-treater's delight
from out that primal night of prowling fears:

Now,
Expressions withered to a wicked mirth,
they refuse, like ghosts, to depart this Earth,
entropy swelling each to monstrous girth,
wearing leers no candle would dare to light:
orange watchers shedding fat slugs for tears.

When Black Tom Came

Old Black Tom's out rutting amid the vild stones—
ululate passion, he mates on mounds of elder bones.
That black billy-goat's tri-horned crown
his triple-eyes, & hooves subtle as eiderdown
his high, hypnotic, yet guttural bray
haunt these wastelands of primordial clay.

Those gaunt people of the village mutter
that his displeasure sours new-churned butter—
that his third eye is a demoniacal orb
desirous of human suffering to absorb.
In fear, they leave offerings on the blighted fallow
& mutter uneasy prayers to appease & hallow.

Black Tom lures she-goats from their pens
& impregnates them out on the reeking fens—
there, amidst menhir & shade-haunted barrow
he cracks old bones to sup on desiccate marrow.
The kids born of Tom's abominable seed
emerge black & blood-hungry, eager to feed.

Fear consumes the village by swift degrees—
Old Black Tom, haughty three-pronged, he sees.
Hunters come to seek his hide, in vain;
they return riven, struck by fever-of-the-brain.
Finally, an altar is reared of immemorial stone
& blood offerings made with a blade of human bone.

But Old Black Tom is not yet satisfied.
Before, it was only she-goats that he plied.
On an eve of wickedly umbric Power
he bleats a beckoning to Pan's bower,
urging the women of the village to come—
they go & copulate with him, each one.

In short order their bellies begin to swell—
the young, the old, all are infested with fell
hybrids that kick cruelly at their distorted wombs.
Out amid the groaning, bone-glutted tombs
Old Black Tom bellows his conquest lewd
while awaiting birth of his degenerate brood.

The Nachzehrer

(inspired by the grave-dwelling, self-devouring revenant of Germanic folklore)

Buried one fortnight in unhallowed earth
following death by poison's burning wrack:
no priest to speak sanctification, dearth
of mournful farewells, of flowers a lack,
swarming flies solely reckoning her worth.

Now eye & jaw gape open wide, her shroud
devoured by famished & slurping degrees,
grave-clothes masticated with munching loud—
hungry for essence of her family,
a bloodline ancient, impious, & proud.

One by one they are stricken to sickness,
growing pale as that sheet she eats below:
no prayer can avert nor patron saint bless
away a hunger which in gorging grows,
lust for lifeforce flowing from her unrest.

As a swine she wings from grave's putrid clutch,
up to St. Stephens, ringing doleful bells
whose tones inflect disease's noxious touch,
pestilence brewing in cistern & well
as rats flee her squeals in writhing bunches.

Too late kinsfolk pretend to lament her
memory, weeping as they disinter
her body from its deep worm-riddled berth,
hoping hint of their ailment to infer
by her cadaver's great gauntness or girth.

See! She has consumed her burial pall,
feasting fat now on her own flesh & blood!
Her own guts she chews, her own bile & gall,
limbs gnawed to bare bone & lips smeared by rud
of a banquet which would a ghoul appall.

Through her jaw a shaft of ashwood driven,
head clean from her shoulders then rudely cleft.
Again she claims what life is her given:
all her kindred fall dead, of blood bereft.
By livid lightning heaven is riven.

Algol's Lamp

By Behenian benison—
hellebore's hex,
high-winking ghoul star—
by thy light sanity unspools.
Unlucky, ill-omened,
glint of reanimate
eye in tomb—
by thy flutter
bones are gnawed
at sepulcher's maw.
Medusa's decapitated
head
by Perseus borne,
thy demon-glare her eye:
catastrophe's flare,
red with were-fire,
blue with dread.
Algol! Thou scar & scare the sky—
beacon of necropoli,
by thy grim Lamp alone
dead of ages restless ply.
Algol!
Star of corpse & crypt,
of coffin-mold &
catacomb—
of candles of cadaver-wax
thou art a lucent wick.

With Sirius
thou vie for
dominance: for
madman's devotion.
High summer his reign,
thy domain Winter's
wrath & torpid motion.
Algol—friend to death,
but luckless to living souls—
thou preside in cairn-yard,
holes fresh-dug & ready to lend—
for all graves empty as
conqueror worm's craw distends.
Algol!
Warden of war,
of unruly passions reaped & sown.
It is said thy stare
will one day strike the whole Cosmos
to stone.

I Must Go

Fall begins briskly & it ends in rot—
what is it that I have forgot?
To light the bright candles—no, no.
My pumpkin's grin already glows.

Perhaps I forgot to appease the dead,
restless & rotting in their coffin-beds?
But no—my offerings are all laid out.
It is not this I have forgot about.

Bright leaves roar like living flame
as they glorify in Autumn's fame:
full moon ascends, a garish glaring red.
The trees are gilded, as if they bled.

Is all our harvest brought in at last?
Winds howl, a chilling specter cast
from out furthest Hyperborean north:
cold will rule these lands henceforth.

See, the straw-man trembles too:
all meddlesome crows long ago flew.
Gourd-guardian of fallow earth,
he reigns over death as he did at birth.

Fields are swathed in a spectral mist—
have I locked all doors, my crucifix kissed?
Something unseen at the window scratches:
a rogue spirit up from those blighted patches.

I know I have forgot some vital thing.
Witches cackle, high on the Hunter's wing.
Huddling down, I whisper fearful prayers,
yet the monist God remains unawares.

Instead, Cernunnos hears my plea,
& pipes rejoinder in reedy melody.
My blood froths as his alluring call
summons me forth to Black Mab's ball.

Tonight the Horned God dies anew:
his ichor the dead earth shall renew.
Spilled at slaying, his seed will bring
about pale snowdrops of early Spring.

Briskly, I adorn myself in dew.
Like gemstones gleam moon's residue.
With reddish berries I stain my skin,
soul surrendered to a bewitching sin.

Fall begins briskly & it ends in rot—
what is it that I have forgot?
Never now will I in surety know:
the Great Night beckons, & I must go.

Forbidden Fruit

Forbidden fruit distending from lustrous vine—
about my feet restless creepers twine.
Upwards peering, gape-mouthed & eyed,
all semblance of self-preservation belied
by the transfixing meat & sumptuous rind
of that fruit with which each vine is lined.

Faceted like gems plundered from nobleman's tomb,
each fruit bulges from a hypnotically wavering bloom;
the flowers emit a lulling, insouciant attar
which shears the mind from its crude husk of matter.
Thus transported, one stands in helpless rapport
whilst hungry tendrils apply their digestive spore.

In this shade-bower, riddled with bones,
I release an ecstatic succession of moans
as the beauteous fruit falls into my hand:
I take a bite in surrender to supernal command.
Its taste is sweet, unbearable, divine,
ardor of infernal suns refined on the vine.

I shiver as my skin dissolves into green-yellow foam,
nostrils choked with scent of sentient loam.
Fruit-borne bliss sours, a malignant daydream,
as I part half-liquid lips to gurgle a scream.
But too late: I am seized by vines' verdurous hold
& must soon join my kin in the omnipotent mould.

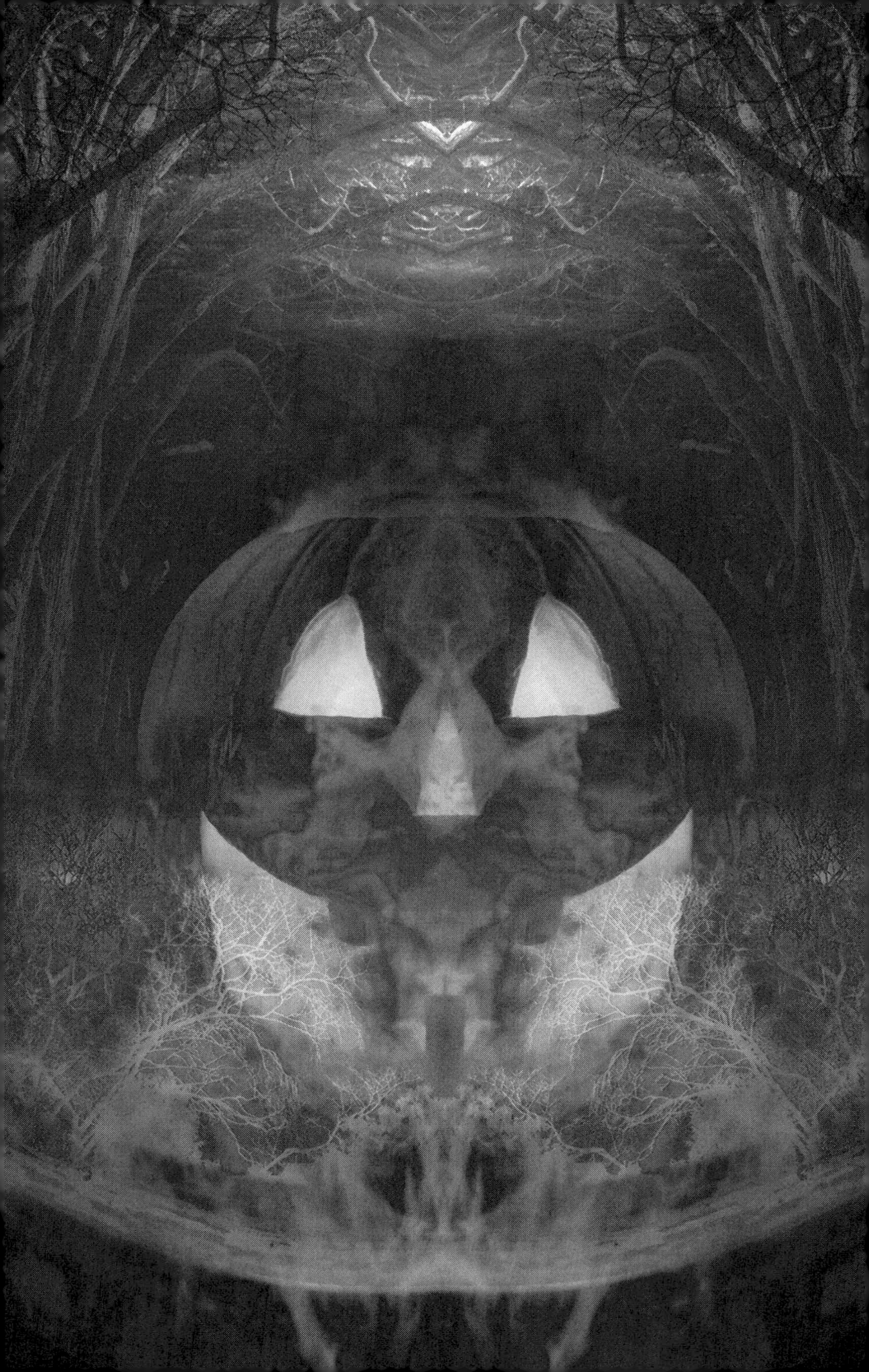

On Hallowe'en

Joining witches in astral flight,
I lie in waking wonderment.
Viewing visions beyond mere sight,
soul from bosom blissfully rent!

Tincture of mandrake-root & gall:
bonfires ignite to twilit rites.
'Neath October's Autumnal pall
we writhe & gape at hallowed frights.

Wend of seasons to Summer's end,
crux of crossroads 'twixt birth & blight.
To this dim path all roadways bend,
lit by sad shade & flitting sprite.

The fate of Jack is surely mine:
to some a bane, to me Divine.
Cursed to wander ever through night
with this lone lantern as my light,
a wan & wonder-stricken wight.

Part 5

A Crown of Seasons

January, I am Come

January, I am come—
to see what is new in this world.
To see what ice-crust
& acorn-husk have to
offer. Your sun—so vivid
in a snow-plied sky!
All the earth is pupil
to your eye.

January, I am come—
to taste old fruits again.
To converse with ageless
rime-crowned angels caught
in blizzard's starry grain.
I am come—& you greet me
at the door, garbed in hoar,
wearing barren grin.

January, I am come—
who has tread your depths
around the sun before
to fathomless regions of space.
A creature new & fantastic
crouches by year's door:
something of sublimity
graven on its face.

Tithe for February

February—the underbelly
of any year.
You come creeping loveless,
breathless in fear—
the cold strikes like an asp
as throats toil & rasp.

February—you slither like
a frost-snake
from the coals of January,
scales of ashen-flake.
Trees tremble at your blast—
life's dominion passed.

Yet—see that hint of sun's
new turning?
By luminous sliver its orb
longer burning—
day by day light's ardent advance
troubles Winter's solemn trance.

Still deep—with howling snows
that stoic blow
to mound about tree-bole & grave.
The flakes fall slow,
somnolent & gorged, to earth:
relinquish themselves to birth

Great crystalline waves of
whelming white.
The green world conquered,
warmth set to flight:
sky a drear & sullied skein
ripe with wracks of frozen rain.

February—what words of praise
can frigid lips
utter to your ice-clad mien?
Coy-cocked hips
bound in cincture of rime—
flesh a slurried slime.

In your underbelly the year
germinates, awakes,
contemplating the upcoming
Summer's stakes.
Bulbs yearn to burst & crest
like corpses never laid to rest—

Yet, the wayward robin dreams
of weaving nests
as sap solidifies to furthest sleep,
Winter's test reigning still o'er height & deep—
unconquered bastions of its keep.

On a Northern March

March—piecemeal you come.
From Winter's fetters barely sprung—
& still sinus-cavity & lung
feel the Old Man's monstrous bite.

March—you reside in snow & soil,
in the soul's straining & bitter toil
towards Springtime's too-enticing foil.
Yet—rime abounds, & mounds of white.

March—there is in you something heavy,
ponderous & ominous, a swollen levee,
ground gravid, but bare the limbs of tree—
fruition of life itself yet a shade.

March—you chase hares into their holes.
There they stew, mutter madness to moles.
In fields frost greets the new-born foal—
on withered-brown & dead ground laid.

March—the sun girdles your spare belt.
Wind & wuther you wear as a pelt.
In slight susurrant gusts the change is felt—
blood stirring in sympathy with sap.

March—birdsong returns, day by day,
poking pinholes in your mantle of gray.
Leaves embalm the land in rank decay:
loam eager for tread of Jack Greencap.

March—you promise, entice, enchant!
Freedom from cold your eloquent cant.
Sunbeams dapple your dressage, slant
like spears to prickle at Winter's hide.

Yet, the Old Man's skin is tough as stone—
& still must sunlight pierce his bone.
Refuses he yet to relinquish your throne:
March, in toilsome servitude must you abide.

April's Aegis

Regeneration emergent from dross—
sun dapples gaily on greening moss.
Winter's mold is broke in twain:
leaves usher ardent along windy lanes,
celebrant at the Old Man's loss.

April's aegis dawns fair & keen—
squirrels scrabble furiously to glean
stores secreted in knot-hole & soil:
due arrears for their Autumnal toil.
Barren ground basks in sunlit sheen.

Pockets of arctic air yet stir,
nettlesome as a tenacious burr:
gray wraps of rainfall array the sun,
from the netherworld his freedom won.
Before Spring's green switch flees Winter's cur.

April!—you hint at new works undone,
at fresh skeins in need of being spun.
Spiders scurry, heed the weaver's call,
knitting webs to hold Death itself in thrall—
life ascendant as entropy reels in stun.

Raiment of vigor drapes the racing hare
as snowdrops unfurl their pallid flare:
soon trillium will grace the forest lanes
with ghosts of pearlescent & purple flame.
Trees stretch & blossom, brood & stare.

April!—you are the fulgent burning bud
arising wild o'er wastes of fecund mud.
Your stride shakes the cold-struck earth,
footsteps seeding spore, stimulating birth—
you sup on sap & quick-running blood.

Now rolls the wheel in relentless motion—
April—sacrosanct—yours is Nature's devotion!
Green sprawls in reverence to spawning self
as ice withdraws its muting, mantling shelf.
April—the egg hatches, yolk in locomotion.

May's Garland

May's garland laid on brow of Earth:
soil hot with birth.
Flowers burn in coronation's glory,
banishing the hoary
breath of Winter's too-patient dearth.

Freshets of Spring flow in jubilation,
life a libation
poured over loam thirsty with cold—
the Old Man's mold
cracked by Nature's lush incantation.

Verdant vines twine from arbor & hedge,
growth a swift sledge
drawn by sylvan elves in ecstatic rush—
cheeks greening blush
& speckle with florets blue of sedge.

Change in air, in sap, in addled blood,
succor of sunlight's flood—
spirits stimulate in tree-bole & breast
as fragrant winds attest
to bowers effulgent up from sterile mud.

May's garland drapes the queenly crest
of Summer's zest,
warm nights raucous with twilit chatter
of insect matters,
gloaming with murmurous mantras blest:

Waxing the day-fires, hours flushed long
with bright birdsong—
Green Men grin as the Wicker Man
burns to fan
flames of herbage in flourishing throng.

Ebullience, elation, joyful exclamation—
May's expectation
laves Winter's rime-rust from the soul,
making all whole
& absolving Hades' toll of reclamation.

June's Bloom

Spring's candle flares to Summer's flame—
destined to spark fair Autumn's pyre.
Up-thrust sheaves of gold & green disdain
death to stoke waves of flourishing fire.

June's bloom bursts forth in fragrant war—
air flush with tufts of spore & seed.
Sunlight penultimate turns to gore
amid clouds that, come evening, bleed

with roseate stain of Summer's awe!
No cold breath or coy tongue of frost
violates Helios' voluptuous law:
Winter a pale & presenceless ghost.

June's bloom exudes exuberant joy,
each laving wind a lover's caress—
sunbeams smite a sovereign alloy
from dross on Nature's anvil blest.

Fae muster as Midsummer nears;
from Mab's court flowing in droves
to swell the berry & crown the deer,
paint the pastures & anoint the groves.

Now dawns the longest, most fulgent day—
Sun garbs himself in glories of fame.
Warmth imbues blood & inert clay
in measures equal: one the other became.

June! You flow like wine into a cup
filled to bejeweled brim: your blaze
warms bones rime-addled, lifts up
hearts slushy & sodden: your rays

pierce Poets to the greening's quick!
No rest amid flower & leaf & mold:
Summer must first wax fever-sick
before coming of Winter's curative cold.

July's Delight

July—hot enough to dry
my quill.
Sunlight's rill raises waves
to ripple lazily;
lawns crowned with sere
& yellowed stalk.

July—sun's eye sees
busy mazes of bees.
Flowers droop languid
in heat-lust—dust
rises to crown each
cooling gust.

July—seat of summer,
Sol's altar, torrid mummer.
In indolent sway of sweat
& succulence; fruit
green-fulgent on vine,
air sticky-dense.

July—Ra's rumination.
Rains kiss earth to life's
elation. Creation throngs
in hedge, microcosmic
cosmos in flower-song—
mosquitoes mutter
bloodletting's pledge.

July—hot enough to dry
my quill.
Ink powder-parched by
sunbeam's spill—you are
sick, ill with yourself,
reveling yet unwell.

July—swathes of
humid night define the
underbelly of your light.
Fierce & foul,
fair & strong, thronging
with solar might—

Cicada's hum comes to
drowse away your bright daze
of delight.

The Crown of August

The crown of August comes crushing
the beaded wheat to bread—
the bright fruit & shaded herbage
& lazy hustle to prepare for
Winter's still-distant bed.

Golden glow the teeming furrows
swollen with Summer's yield—
thick-set stems & drowsing flowers
bow before Lugh's tumid spear,
ripe-rich rays bathing gravid fields.

Now the days grow shorter, shorter:
night a looming, chilling shade.
Apples radiate on gnarled branches
as cicadas trill indolent, each
tang of grass gorged to fulsome blade.

To stab at the hardening heart
of Autumn seems yet within bounds—
too hot still the days & nights,
hay-scent biting on the wind,
air vibrant with aureate sights & sounds.

Yet—the Northern breath is present
in every evening undercurrent—
Oh sweet animus of Summer!
You will go 'neath the reddening leaves
like a beggar in crimson rags rent.

September's Specter

In September comes the specter
of rot & creeping mold:
The wind, rank with Summer's breath,
exhales undercurrents of cold.

Chill dawns bathe fulsome gardens
where blight shows on the stem:
Fruits fall to rupture on withered loam
as August withdraws her aureate hem.

Wannish shine the ever-earlier evenings
wherein spirits creep & stalk:
In riming twilight elf-utterance flows
in silvern rhythms of rhyming mock.

They laugh at the newly wilted fronds
of High Summer's queenly crown:
At nascent buddings too-late sprung
they growl & jeer & fret & frown.

In September stirs the sun-weary Earth
to receive Autumn's sacrifice:
The inverse of April's exuberant birth.
Men gather in wheat like mice.

See the stalks lean heavy, nodding
beneath rotten blossoms, deep
in the somnolence of perishing plants,
a subtle & sickly-sour sleep.

Soon the snows will come to loosen
the ligature of all Nature's ties:
Beneath a coat of killing adamant drifts
the seed slumbers, the insect dies.

O September, thou specter still green-flushed
with the final drops of Summer's blood!
The berry is full, the corn towering & lush:
Leaves blush, precipitate a falling flood.

October's Gate

When the gourd curdles on the vine
& hoar-grapes are plucked for winter wine—
winds gust, torrents of gray
wafting incarnadine leaves at play.

The hearth is kindled, not to be out-blown
until Spring has its cruel kindness shown.
Without, green things grow rot-mottled:
within, life & light are refined & bottled.

A smell of baking pies: the roaring fire
becomes in its kindling Summer's pyre.
A few reeking, languid days of heat
yet haunt the Autumn's imperial creep.

Nights wax, until a perpetuate shade
is cast on each bent & browned grass-blade—
easy season of life stumbles to a halt
as Winter stirs in its sepulchral vault.

Too, there are stirrings in the soil:
the dead choose this season to relax, uncoil.
To wander by a graveyard at dusk
is to invite the scenting of spectral musk.

Or perhaps, a phantom may be seen:
thin & pallid or ghoulish & green.
The shivering shells of atrophied leaves
heap in bouquets on graves no-one grieves.

At Hallowe'en heathens mark year's end:
the first day Summer can no more defend.
The veil, a corpse-shroud, is rent in twain,
freeing the exanimate to inhabit Earth again.

From every stoop burns a carven smile—
pumpkin-play holds at bay the guile
of undead visitants in the month-long night.
The dark is fraught with ancestral fright.

October, open wide your haunted gates—
the sun is setting, the harvest is late.
As a traveler on a bone-pale road
your leaf-crowned avatar hauls his load
to some snug & silent Winter abode:
beyond lies the ailing year's fatal fate.

November in Rags

November, you come with snows.
Glinting powder mounds & grows
in lieu of flowers:
At midnight a moon-jewel glows
between frost-fretted bowers.

The black tomb has more grace—
the corpse, enlivened by lace
seems more vital.
From the sun you avert your face,
a season bleak & ghoulishly idle.

What harbinger of too-distant Spring
can these sable winds solemnly bring?
There is no bloom but ice:
Here, the old year's atrophy clings
with subtlety of an iron vice.

Candles flare in window-panes
as Winter paves each weary lane:
Clouds roil drear,
draping their fumarole stain
over the gaunt carcass of the year.

Beneath this pall, unshed leaves chatter
as gales their perilous bastion batter:
Vacant fields gape
at the sky's soot-defiled tatter,
each cloud mounded to monstrous shape.

November, you come with snows:
Life trembles before your leaden blows.
Beyond lies Yule's light:
But first must you pluck Summer's rose
to gild with the fetid pith of night.

December's Augury

December! Lights & drums
define your phantasmal form.
Snow settles—unwelcome, yet
easing.
Gray introspection becomes
the nodding Poet's norm.

Fires flare beyond window-
panes, evergreens decked in
pagan array: a muffling circlet
of snowfall
girds the earth, guarding seeds.
Skyward stalks Orion, hale & thin.

December's augury is cast:
what will the coming year offer
or forfend? Black winds of arctic
ardor
blast the naked limbs of tree
& Man alike, mere clothing no buffer.

Spirits wail on the night-wind,
scratch sigils in fanning frost:
old songs are poured forth from
new skins,
warming rites of angelic prayer
working to thwart Winter's will embossed.

Divine what form the cinders take
as the Yule-fire expires, futures seen:

the ash-dusted ember mutters its need,
dying.
Without, crisp snow coats gravestones in
tombing mantles of diamond sheen.

December! Last stop before the year
pales to a ghost who forever haunts
the mind: obsolete calendars are eyed warily,
wearily.
Ice coalesces in carapaces on
all things, rendering reality cadaver-gaunt.

Ahead, the New Year: ahead, the road
wending to fresh, unstitched time.
We mark December's death in blood, hot—
sunlight a specter warmly remembered,
present world a womb of killing rime.

About the Contributors

SCOTT J. COUTURIER is a poet and prose writer of the Weird, liminal, & darkly fantastic. His work has appeared in numerous venues, including *The Audient Void*, S. T. Joshi's *Spectral Realms*, *Eye To The Telescope*, *The Dark Corner Zine*, *Space and Time Magazine*, and *Weirdbook*. Currently, he works as a copy and content editor for Mission Point Press, living an obscure reverie in the wilds of northern Michigan with his partner/live-in editor & two cats. His short story collection, *The Box*, was published in 2022 by Hybrid Sequence Media. His second collection of poetry, which focuses on cosmic horror, is forthcoming from Jackanapes Press.

REBECCA BUCHANAN is the editor of the Pagan literary ezine, *Eternal Haunted Summer*, and is a regular contributor to *evoke: witchcraft*paganism*lifestyle*. Her work has appeared in a variety of venues, and her poems have been nominated for the Pushcart Prize and the Dwarf Star Award. Her poem "Heliobacterium daphnephilum" won the Rhysling Award in 2020. She has released four short story collections and two poetry collections: *A Witch Among Wolves, and Other Pagan Tales* (Asphodel Press); *The Serpent in the Throat, and Other Pagan Tales* (Asphodel Press); *The Fox and the Rose, and Other Pagan Faerie Tales* (Asphodel Press); *Asphalt Gods, and Other Pagan Urban Fantasy Tales* (Asphodel Press); *Dame Evergreen, and Other Poems of Myth, Magic, and Madness* (Sycorax Press); and *Not a Princess, But (Yes) There Was a Pea, and Other Fairy Tales to Foment Revolution* (Jackanapes Press). Her occult adventure novella, *The Secret of the Sunken Temple*, and her short story collection, *North of Sun, South of Moon, and Other Pagan Myths and Faerie Tales*, are forthcoming from Sigil House Productions.

DAN SAUER is a graphic designer and artist living in Oregon. In 2016, he co-founded (with editor/publisher Obadiah Baird) *The Audient Void: A Journal of Weird Fiction and Dark Fantasy*, which features his design and illustration work. Since 2017, he has worked extensively on book covers and interior art for Hippocampus Press and other publishers. His art often takes the form of surreal collage and photomontage, as pioneered by artists such as Max Ernst, Wilfried Sätty, Harry O. Morris

Made in the USA
Columbia, SC
23 September 2022